Move Your Chair

Chair

A Guide to

Every Day Excellence

What to, How to, Why to

Rick Weinheimer

Move your Chair

Published October 2015

CreateSpace Independent Publishing Platform

Front cover photo and design: Thanks to Rachel McCarver and Jeff Metz, two skilled teachers and artists, and to student Paige Grider

Back cover photo: Courtesy of Molly Connor

ISBN-13: 978-1516934669

ISBN-10: 1516934660

This book is dedicated to all mentors, especially these three:

Dr. Leonard Lawton (Doc)

Coach Marshall Sellers (Marsh)

and, most of all,

Mr. Allan Weinheimer (Dad)

Table of Contents

Foreword: Discovering Every Day

Having loved distance running in high school, I couldn't imagine my college experience without running cross-country and track, despite the fact that I had not been recruited by any college coaches. I discovered a small college in the Midwest (DePauw University in Greencastle, Indiana), known for outstanding academics but, more importantly for me, known for having an open policy for its running program.

How excited I was to put on that black and gold uniform, to lace up my spikes, and to toe the starting line with my new collegiate teammates. Pretty amazing, right?

How about this for the result? My freshman year in cross-country I finished last in every race I ran. My results in track were very similar.

As track season ended in May, I decided that I didn't like finishing last and that I was going to try to do something about it. Lacking any external guidance, I devised my own plan to improve. That plan began with my running five

1

miles at whatever pace I could handle. Every single day.

Two weeks later, I progressed to running seven miles. Every day.

A month after that, I moved up to ten miles. Every day.

By mid-July I felt this "every day approach" working. Excited, I telephoned our coach and told him that I would really be ready for our team running camp that would open the season in the fall.

He dampened my excitement. "Rick," (though he had learned my name, he would always spell it wrong; it was "Ric" for the next three years) he said, "We have several freshmen who will be joining the team this year. I don't anticipate that there will be room for you to come to camp with us."

I felt a big letdown, kind of sick to my stomach. So I ran twice that day, and I kept on running. Every day.

As it turned out, there was just enough room for me to attend the camp. While everyone else was provided a cot to sleep on at night, all that was left for me to sleep on was a big piece of foam rubber. It wasn't level, so I would keep rolling off of it into the grass while I was trying to sleep. But at least I had a spot, and I wanted to make the most of it.

On the first day of camp, after receiving our physical exams at the Health Center, Coach told us to run from our school gymnasium along the highway all the way to the campgrounds thirteen miles away. Sleeping bags and gym bags were loaded onto a bus that would travel behind us. We all lined up, including our returning senior All-American runner, along with our other veterans and the new freshmen. Our coach, all 5'2" and 112 pounds of him with a voice that sounded like he'd been sucking helium from a balloon, leaned out the driver's window of a pale gold station wagon that would lead the way. Coach yelled a high-pitched "Go!" And we all took off.

With my summer of training every day within me and with the adrenaline rush of wanting to show Coach that I belonged with the group, I took off running fast, faster than everyone else. I started faster, but not smarter. Typical August day in Indiana, sunny, about 90 degrees, and thick humidity. The other runners set an intelligent pace for weather that warm. I didn't think; I just ran, right to the front. I ran just as I had all summer.

At each mile mark Coach was parked by the side of the road where he would shout in his squeaky voice how many miles I had covered. Never looking back at my teammates, I felt great for the first five or six miles. By mile seven, the humidity was closing in on me, squeezing my face, constricting my breathing. By mile eight I was drenched in perspiration; not a spot on my running shorts was dry. Coach squeaked from the side of the road, "Eight miles!" And he climbed back into his car.

By mile nine I knew I was in trouble. I couldn't keep the sweat out of my eyes. Too fast, too soon, too hot, too humid. I cursed myself mentally. I had really wanted to show everyone how much I had improved. With heavy legs and a cloudy mind, closing in on mile ten I started stumbling. I couldn't go any farther. The disappointment was heavier than my legs.

I spotted the parked station wagon and plodded up behind it. I stopped, bent over with my hands on my knees. My chest heaved. Coach said, "Ten miles."

I stammered, "I'm...sorry...Coach. That's all...I can...do."

He nodded.

Discouraged, I stood up and waited for the rumbly school bus to pull up on the dusty shoulder behind me. I watched the doors slide open while wondering if any of my teammates were already riding, if any of them had stopped like me. I prayed I wasn't going to be the only one on that bus.

It took all my remaining effort to lift my sweat-saturated Adidas running shoes as I climbed those three steps. I looked up the aisle to find a seat to collapse into, and I was confused by what I saw. My mind cleared. I realized that every one of my teammates was already sitting on the bus. Everyone had stopped before mile seven because of the intense heat. For the last three miles, they had been ambling along, waiting for me to be finished.

As I slowly moved down the aisle to find a seat, our All-American reached over and patted me on the shoulder.

I didn't tell you this story because I became an Olympic runner, or a world record holder, or anything. I'm just a normal person. During our racing season that fall, our All-American always beat me, as did two or three of our other guys.

I told the story because it is something you need to know about me to understand what I am sharing with you in this book. You need to understand why I believe in applying your efforts to do your best.

Every day.

Since that time I've been intrigued with "excellence" and with successful people. Now, as a high school English teacher and coach for almost forty years, I've observed many successful people in my life, and I've studied many famously successful people. I've wanted to learn not only the "what" they've achieved but also the "how" and the "why" they've achieved it, the product, the process, and the purpose.

This book is about striving for excellence in your life, whether you consider yourself to be blue collar or white collar, whether you are currently a homemaker or a home builder, whether you are still in high school planning your future or you are already living that future.

This book is about the process of seeking excellence in any area. It will provide pragmatic tips for your own life and for the lives of those you influence, formally or informally, as a family member, a parent, a teacher, a coach, a counselor, or a mentor. This book is for you, whatever age, place, or situation you are in, if you want to strive for excellence.

This is what I mean by that word.

Excellence: Achieving at the highest level possible over a long period of time.

Every day.

Chapter 1: Everyday vs. Every Day

Excellence is an elusive goal for many people. The pathway there is winding and rutted and difficult to follow. People wonder if they have the tools, the abilities, the appropriate maps, and the right determination to get there.

Our world is constantly evolving in ways that make achieving excellence even more challenging. Our world spins faster and faster with more activity crammed into our schedules than ever before. The expectation from our bosses, from our teachers, and most powerfully from ourselves is that we achieve at high levels and then push ourselves higher and further. Then why don't we achieve excellence?

Changes swirl around us. Technology grows exponentially daily. As I sit here at my typewriter—not really—I know that my MySpace account is becoming obsolete as are all my connections on Facebook, Twitter, Instagram,

Snap Chat, and FutureBlog (Okay, I made that last one up).

No wonder we feel overwhelmed.

Our whirlwind world that often leaves us breathless, and that just as often may leave us feeling empty, has pushed us into a situation where we must not be controlled by life but rather take control of our lives. We can sort it all out. We can understand excellence, and we can seek it out in the areas of our lives that are the most important to us.

That's why this book has been written.

As I said, I've always been intrigued by excellence and those who seem to have achieved it. As a coach, I knew I wanted my teams to achieve at a high level, and I knew I needed the right approach to get them there, so I began by studying Vince Lombardi, the legendary football coach of the Green Bay Packers. Lombardi reportedly once said, "Winning isn't everything. It's the only thing." What a great aphorism—succinct, memorable, and (as this English teacher appreciates) parallel in its syntax. The Lombardi quote appears on posters, and it's been repeated countless times. It's an easy line to drop into a pre-competition pep talk, and it feels good because we all love winning.

Just one problem with it though: it's not true.

Winning is not the only thing and believing that it is will not lead you to excellence. I realized this when thinking about the measure for excellence for the cross-country teams I coach: earning medals at the state cross-country finals. The top five finishing teams of the 400+ that start the tournament are rewarded by being recognized and led up onto our awards platform. The crowd roars, and the runners who are introduced by name have medals placed around their necks. Parents and photographers elbow their way to the front and snap pictures. It is a scene of color, noise, energy, and excitement.

Runners are on the awards stand for about six minutes.

That fact is what made the "winning is the only thing" philosophy fail for me because over the course of the year between trips to the awards platform, our runners have run every day or almost every day. Our girls have typically each logged over 14,000 minutes of running (which would be about ten full days if someone ran 24/7), and our boys have usually each run over 21,000 minutes (every minute for over two weeks) in preparation for the state championships. Fourteen to twenty-one thousand minutes...all to enjoy the six minutes of "winning" on the awards stand? Winning can't be the only thing. Winning has to be about all that has gone into those thousands of minutes of preparation and all the growth that has come from that dedication.

When I realized that, I knew I had discovered the path toward excellence. I also knew that if I could put it into words, I could help others who wanted excellence in any of its forms in their own lives. As I read further about successful people, I discovered that, no matter what area their success had come in, their achievement occurred, like a last place runner determined to improve, as a result of their efforts each and every day.

When I type "every day" into this manuscript, my automatic spell check wants to change it into one word "everyday." But that's not what I want this to say. As a single word, "everyday" means "ordinary, normal, and of no distinction." As two words, "every day" is actually the opposite: "extraordinary, distinctive, and significant" because that's the kind of effort it takes to achieve at the highest level. Few people choose to apply themselves to their goals, their purposes, and their achievements every single day. Few are willing to find that level of focus.

How "every day" can someone be? The answer to that connects to another question: How "every day" can three siblings be? Here is the story of one family.

The older brother Tim, now thirty-three years old, began running daily on Christmas Day 1999 and hasn't missed a single day in almost sixteen years. The middle child, sister Kerilyn now twenty-eight, decided, "If Tim can do it, I can do it!" and she has run every day for thirteen and a half years. Twenty-seven year old Michelle, the youngest, was not planning to be a runner at all, but when she wasn't selected for the high school volleyball team, she decided to put her energy into cross-country. She began running that very day and has run every day of the twelve years since.

In spite of the fact that they are siblings, Tim, Kerilyn, and Michelle have no genetic gift that has given them the ability to run every day. They just find a way, and before you know it, twelve or thirteen or sixteen years have passed. They celebrate milestone moments, a big party for the ten-year anniversary or a 5K family race to commemorate running day number 5000, but generally it is an internal decision to lace on their running shoes each day and then do it again the next day. New acquaintances are often amazed at the accomplishment and react with "I don't think there's anything I have ever done for twelve (or thirteen or sixteen) years." Kerilyn's reply: "It's not even a choice anymore. Doing this every day has become a part of who we are."

Whether you choose to run, or play the piano, or pray, or praise your children, or participate in community service, or even brush your teeth, there is power and potential in taking an every day approach.

That's why this book exists.

Keep reading to learn about how to push back against the world around you, a world in which for many people "ordinary" is sufficient and "everyday" (one word) is enough. Instead, learn to take charge of pursuing the excellence you want and to become an "every day person." The result is transforming, and you can learn to enjoy the control of your life in new ways.

What this book has for you are specific philosophies you can create, specific decisions you can make, and specific actions you can take. All of which are designed to help you seek excellence in the areas of your life that are most important to you, using the process of "every day excellence."

Many examples will come from my world-- teaching and coaching--because that's my realm of experience. You can apply those to whatever your world is and to wherever you want to experience excellence—in business, or parenting, or relationship building, or schooling, or your spirituality.

Waiting for you after the final chapter will be a series of guided planning sheets that will help you structure a plan of action. What you can do and how you can do it...starting right away.

You will learn to see the pursuit of excellence as a process, a journey, an adventure, and then how to train yourself to follow that quest, and to include a compassionate outlook every single day.

Chapter 2: A Negative Times a Negative Is NOT a Positive

One day Elijah, one of my athletes, said to me, "Coach, I have a question. You're able to tell us about literature and running and training and racing and life. I've just been wondering: How do you know so much?"

Elijah didn't really intend that as a compliment, though I chose to take it that way (you take compliments wherever you can get them!) He really meant it as a question, so I will try to answer it. I've been an English teacher and a distance running coach for thirty-eight years. Each day at school I observe, work alongside, or interact with over 2,000 people. Doing the math: 2000 people x 180 days a year x 38 years=over 13,680,000 (13.68 million) contacts with people. (You can check that math, but I'm pretty confident. My dad was a math teacher.) Just by observation you can learn a lot of lessons from 13 million contacts with people.

So the answer to Elijah was this: "If I know a lot, it's because I've had the opportunity to learn from a lot of different people." The ideas in this book come from observations, the processing of those observations, and the desire to understand the stages of pursuing excellence.

I want to add this disclaimer as you read on: my wife Amy has a rule that after someone reaches the age of 50, he no longer must have a filter; he can say whatever he wants to say. I'm 59 years old, and I plan to make liberal use of that rule!

First of all, we need to be aware of what surrounds us if we want to exercise some control over our lives. What surrounds us is a difficult world, one where the negative side greatly outweighs the positive in our daily interactions. This has developed for a variety of reasons: safety, habit, routine, technological advances, disillusionment, cynicism. We must understand this and be aware of this if we expect to experience some control in our world.

There are various reasons why the negative surrounds us, and you can probably come up with three or four without putting in too much thought. For example, how often is a young child told "no"? Hundreds of times? Thousands? Even more?

No, don't touch that socket.

No, stay away; the stove is hot.

No, don't put that toad in your mouth.

As you can see, the foundation for the negative begins very early in our lives with our parents and caregivers keeping us safe from many problematic situations. The result is that the first language lesson of our lives and the first word of power we learn is the word "No!"

Like anyone else, a child wants some control of his environment. Having learned this language lesson, young children often say "no" even when they mean "yes" because they understand the word's power.

Our granddaughter Grace was fascinating to watch as she developed language. Pint-sized and pigtailed, she often clung tenaciously to the power of the word "no." A linguist in Pampers, she used language as a tool to control her world, often saying "no" even when she wanted to answer "yes."

"Grace, do you want to go for a walk?"
"No!"

"Grace, do you love Pop?"
"No!"

"Grace, do you want ice cream?"
"No!"

Of course she has grown out of that stage, as most of us do ("most," not "all",) but it really demonstrated that she understood the power of language and perhaps the strongest word in English: No.

Think of the impact of that lesson on all of us. No wonder we have a foundation in negativity.

As we grow older, we learn another lesson. When we do something right, we get praised for it. If we do that same right thing again, we get less praise for it. If we do it a third time, we may get no praise at all. Conversely, when we do something wrong, we get negative feedback. If we do the same wrong thing again, the feedback is even more negative. If we do that same thing a third time, look out!

Slowly, and perhaps naturally, the negative grows to dominate our lives because it draws the most attention. How many graded papers are returned to you when you are in school? What answers are marked for your attention? Of course. The wrong ones in most cases. You are immediately aware of the negative. Invariably this process causes you to focus on your mistakes. It would be a rare occurrence in a classroom for a student who gets 97 out of 100 correct on a test to tell a classmate, "Give me a few minutes. I want to read through all the answers I got right." Instead, students immediately focus on their mistakes. This is just another example of the pervasiveness of the negative.

By the time they reach high school, students are often stuck in the negativity that surrounds them. Many times I have had a student walk into class at 8:00 am and say, "Mr. Weinheimer, I am having a terrible day!" At 8:00 in the morning they have already labeled it a "terrible day." Usually that label has come because of just one or two things that have gone wrong. Maybe they were getting dressed and got both feet in one leg of their underwear and fell down. Maybe at breakfast their little brother sneezed on their Fruit Loops. Maybe they just didn't get a prime spot in the student parking lot. Because of this one thing and because of the culture of negativity, they are quick to label this as a "terrible day." And how do you think the rest of this day will turn out since they have already proclaimed it terrible?

Most adults can't seem to shake this same pattern, again because of what surrounds them. Over 99% of the stories in the daily newspapers or in the nightly television news is negative. Doesn't it also seem that viewers are lured by negative teasers and negative story lines? Justification from the media is that they are giving the viewers what they want, but isn't it just as likely that viewers are being trained to think they want what they are being given? When I mentioned this fact to a group, Emma, one of the students, made this astute comment: "They start off the news by saying 'Good evening,' and then they promptly go about telling you why it isn't."

The omnipresence (and, sadly sometimes, omnipotence) of social media with great positive potential instead often feeds the negativity in our culture. Dangerous because it is instantaneous and often anonymous, social media has contributed trolling and catfishing, Facebook bullying, angry Twitter rants, and regrettable Instagram pictures to this world. All this negative energy, natural or self-inflicted, stacks slowly upon itself piece by piece and threatens to fall on us and bury us. And some days it does.

This pervasive negativity is the reason that some people react to life the way that a convenience store clerk reacted one morning. I had stopped on my way to school to pick up a donut, and when I checked out at the register, the clerk mumbled, "How're you today?"

He didn't expect an answer. It was just a way to fill the silence. Or perhaps his boss had instructed him to ask. But I was excited about the day, and so I decided to answer truthfully: "I'm doing great!" And then I decided to push the issue: "How're *you* doing?"

The clerk stopped a moment as if he didn't expect the question. His eyebrows narrowed. He cleared his throat. My donut sat expectantly on the counter. Finally, he said, "Well, I'll be great...once I get out of this place."

As I was driving off, I thought about his answer. Then I decided to do the math about his situation, partly because I've found I can always do math better when I'm eating a donut. That man works 40 hours a week, 50 weeks a year, a 40-year career. That's 80,000 hours. That's 80,000 hours spent thinking, "I'll be great when I get out of here."

What a sad waste of time, energy, and life. But I suggest that this clerk is not all that different from many other people, people who are thinking life will get better once they get out of a current situation. The negativity around us is quicksand that slowly sucks us under. Before we know it, we feel powerless to escape.

That prevailing negativity manifests itself in many ways. One morning I came into school to see that overnight a student had anonymously put sticky post-it notes on 100 lockers, all with positive sayings on them.

"You can do it!"

"Reach your potential!"

"Someone cares about you!"

While I was smiling at this effort, a colleague came up beside me and said, "Oh, great. Who is going to pick all those up when they fall off the lockers?"

How inundated with the negative had he become when he would instantly think of a problem with 100 positive notes? What has happened to us? How widespread is this feeling?

I have been there too. Early in my teaching career I kept a poster hanging in my room that said, "Have you ever had one of those *lives* where nothing seems to go right?" At the time it seemed kind of cynically funny. Now it seems awkwardly defeating. What message was that poster sending to the students?

And what message was I sending to the runners that I coached? Three days a week before school at 6:00 am, our distance runners practice. Early in my career, I dreaded every one of those morning runs because I wasn't a "morning person." I knew I wasn't a morning person because when I was young, I often woke up cranky, and I remember being told, "Well, you certainly aren't a morning person!"

My parents probably also told me I was handsome, smart, and capable, but for some reason I really remember the not-a-morning-person lesson. I took it to heart, and it would surface in front of the runners at each 6:00 am practice.

The darkness outside seemed overwhelming. I unlocked the gym doors at 5:56, wishing I were still in bed. Runners would stumble in at about 5:58, shoe laces flopping, eyes half-closed, and sporting some seriously frightening hair formations we called "bed head." It was a very solemn time waiting to get started: no talking, no laughing, some runners showing up at the last second, and when practice started, runners plodding along on the run, step by excruciating step. Practice ended and everyone, including the coach, was satisfied just to have survived. Not much was accomplished really, and over time I became frustrated with the lack of passion from the runners. I was looking for a runner who was a "morning person," someone to arrive with energy and enthusiasm, an attitude that would positively influence everyone. I already knew that I couldn't provide that because I wasn't a "morning person."

After many hollow morning practices waiting fruitlessly for the runners to change themselves into enthusiastic participants, I had to face the fact that the only solution to this waste of time was going to have to come from the reluctant coach; that would be me. If we needed energy, I would need to supply it. If we needed enthusiasm, I was going to have to show it. So after giving myself a big pep talk, I showed up about 5:30 the next morning and turned all the lights on in the gym and locker rooms. When runners arrived, I faked being energetic, welcoming them by name. The next day I faked being enthusiastic, smiling and making up jokes about how we all looked first thing in the morning.

Eventually our morning routine began to improve. Runners got to practice earlier, with a little bounce in their now-tied running shoes. They began greeting each other by name, acting happy to see each other, ready to get a fast run in, and our morning practices became full of laughter and energy.

Many years later I still have that voice in my head telling me I'm not a morning person, but at least no one else knows that. (Please keep my secret!) I'm not sure "morning people" really exist, just people who are pretending to be energetic and happy in the morning, but I do know that recognizing the negativity, taking control of that situation, and changing my approach led to much more productive practices. Those practices have led to improved results, and the quest for excellence is in full swing. Positives multiply just as negatives do. This lesson generalizes and applies to the workplace, to family, and to interactions with others.

While some people appear to take delight in spreading negativity, often it is not intentional. Some negative people around us may inadvertently erode our positivity merely because they are ignorant of our efforts to seek excellence. Once I attended a dinner, and a woman at the same table had several questions for me.

"Are you the cross-country coach?"

"Yes," I admitted.

"Why do you require your runners to run every single day?"

Awkward pause. "I don't. I encourage them to use every day that they can to improve."

Then she got to her point. "Well, my nephew is one of your runners, and when we told him we were all going on a family cruise for vacation, he announced to us that he couldn't go

24

unless he could run every day. I just don't see why he would have to run on a vacation."

This woman wasn't intentionally hindering her nephew's every day efforts, yet her ignorance of his commitment to his purpose made things more difficult for him. Fortunately in this case purpose won out over the objections, and the nephew not only ran every day while on the cruise ship, he ran every day that entire calendar year and has kept on going. He has now run over 700 days in a row.

We may have evolved naturally into this negatively-centered world, but it doesn't have to control us if we recognize our circumstances and choose to take specific steps to be distinctly different, to live positively in our negative world.

If you're reading this book, then you can make this change. Be aware of what is around you, and be cognizant of what goes into your brain. You can take control, and you can seek excellence in spite of many negative things in our culture. You can take positive steps, and you can feel the satisfaction that comes with those strides every day.

And you can become a morning person.

Chapter 3: Building your Cathedral

The quest for excellence is not an inter-personal competition; it's an individual journey. You've decided that the negative culture around us, that which naturally has influenced us since we were young, is not going to dominate your life. What else must you decide?

To be distinctly different. On your own journey you must understand you can't be like everyone else. This is what "everyone else" is like:

1. The facilitator of a workshop I once attended began with this statement: "Let's get started on time. That way we can take more breaks, and we can get out early." Many attendees applauded that message. If you're seeking excellence daily, would that opening remark make you excited about the day's workshop? Even worse, what if

getting out early is the highlight of the workshop???

2. Our school newspaper interviewed our top ten academically-ranked students and asked them what advice they would give their classmates. Seven out of ten said something similar to this: "Have more fun." They thought that message might be "cooler" than one about working harder or studying more. There is comfort in being part of the cool crowd. Are you willing to focus on your own journey and not be swayed by others?

3. At every conference I have ever gone to, I have heard at least one attendee say, "If I get one idea from this weekend, this conference has been worth it." Does that illustrate the pursuit of excellence? Are you satisfied with getting only one valuable idea from a three-day conference?

If you have set your expectations higher than what those three situations illustrate, you know you can't be like many of those around you, and you've chosen to read this book. You have decided to take control of your pursuit of excellence, to learn and to act. Here's what you do:

Wake up with a Purpose

Perhaps you've heard this modern "fable." A man walking down the sidewalk comes upon a construction site where one worker is begrudgingly throwing bricks down, moaning and griping. His coworker also has bricks but is putting them strategically in place while humming a happy tune. The observer asks, "What're you guys doing?" The grumpy worker replies, "Can't you see? I'm laying bricks." The cheerful worker smiles and says, "Can't you see? I'm building a cathedral!"

So much of the world around us is based on reaction. Something happens, then we react to it. The next thing happens, then we react to that. Our days are often filled by the pattern: event, reaction, event, reaction, event, reaction, and so on until bedtime. When our heads hit the pillow, we are exhausted and left wondering what, if anything, we have accomplished. Because of the fatigue that accompanies this pattern, our motivation for the next day is minimal. So we wake up and repeat that routine.

This is why if you want to pursue excellence, you must identify your purpose. In the next chapter you will read more about how to do this, but know that waking up with your purpose in mind may be the single most motivating thing you can do. Once you know your purpose, you create the habit of it being the first thing in your mind when your feet hit the floor in the morning.

Creating a cathedral, that's a purpose! Now what will you need to support that purpose?

Show up with an Attitude

You've heard this statistic before with many different percentages: Life is 10% what happens to you and 90% how you react to it. Or 5% and 95%. Or 1% and 99%. The reason you hear that is that the concept itself is correct! The attitude you bring to the events that occur has a huge influence on your reactions.

Unfortunately, you often read that idea without any further explanation about *how* to form the right attitude, and the right attitude doesn't happen magically. The good news is that it isn't innate; it isn't passed down hereditarily, and it isn't in-born. With the right coaching and the right practice, you can develop the attitude you need to support your purpose.

No matter how excited you are about your cathedral, the right attitude will make those bricks easier to lift.

Finish up with a Flourish

One of the biggest sticking points for people who want to seek excellence is that they are unable to keep the focus on their purpose through all the events of a day, or a month, or a year. Things slowly start to unravel and, the next thing they know, they have gone right back to their habitual strategies that didn't work before.

You can push through those sticking points which will enable you to finish up just as strongly as you started. You can become that rare person who is just as focused at the end of the day as at the beginning, just as focused on Friday afternoon as on Monday morning. You don't have a true purpose part of the time; you have your purpose all the time.

You finish with a flourish because you want a beautiful, gleaming spire on the top of your cathedral.

Wrap it up with Compassion

As your purpose brings focus to your day, priority to your decisions, and clarity to your motivation, you will want to have positive impact on those around you, some who will contribute directly to your excellence and others whose contact with you seems to be random or coincidental.

Your intentional choices and actions will affect others and often can motivate or inspire them because most people are not naturally excellence-oriented. Most have a list of reasons (excuses?) not to change. Experience suggests that two forces are at work: the common rationalization for not changing and the equally-common blaming that is directed at others.

Skeptics immediately think of obstacles to this process, some imaginary and some real.

> I don't have the *time*.

> Too many people are asking too much from me.

> I don't have a *mentor*.

> No one will help me.

> I don't have the *self discipline*.

> All my energy goes into being responsible for other people.

> I don't have a big enough *reason to change*.

While these concerns may feel legitimate now, none of these obstacles will interrupt your journey for long if you choose to become an every day person in your pursuit of excellence. Having a new understanding of each of these areas brings a new perspective.

Time: Learning these steps and putting them into your life doesn't actually take any more time out of your day. It just refocuses your time and your day. Much of the thought and planning that goes into it can come during your usual "thinking times" like when you are showering, driving to do your errands, or mowing the lawn.

Mentor: You are holding your mentor in your hands right now—your copy of this book! You may even want to have a friend working on this same process, so there is another built-in support system. The plan pages after the final chapter of this book will help you organize your ideas.

Self discipline: Most of us avoid the term "self discipline" because of its connotation: the process of depriving ourselves of things we really want. It suggests sacrifice, giving up things we want to keep, both physically and emotionally. However, this process of every day excellence is not about giving up anything other than the distractions and often accompanying stress that cloud our days. This is about moving *toward,* not *away from,* things we really want.

A reason to change: Why do you want to work on every day excellence? Because you want to wake up excited about your day. Because you want to replace the negative atmosphere around you with positivity. Because you want to feel more productive. And because you want to go to bed feeling accomplished and prepared for the next day.

Seeing a beautiful cathedral with a gleaming spire that you have built; now, doesn't that sound more exciting than taking longer breaks and getting out early?

Chapter 4: Wake up with a Purpose

Often on the first day of school, I ask my English students to list a number of things about themselves, including three goals or three things they would like to accomplish by the end of the school year. Most students have no idea what to write. They have never thought about what their goals are. They have never thought about what they really want to achieve. Their papers come in blank. This is typical, and not just of teenagers.

Many adults would also have trouble answering some form of that same question: "What would you like to accomplish today?" Adults have a lot of days where they merely follow an agenda, checking items off a To Do list, without much (or any) thought about accomplishment, achievement, or excellence.

Other people may have a goal but no clear strategy for reaching it. Still other people may have a goal, but it is too general or too mainstream instead of being personal and unique.

I fell into that category. For years I, as many other coaches do, had always dreamed of coaching a team that would win a state championship. While we had successful teams for many years, I began to realize how elusive that state championship goal could be. Many factors had to be in place in order to become the single best team. We had to have enough talented runners all in one year. We had to stay injury free. We had to be lucky enough to avoid any freak obstacles, and—most importantly—none of the other 400 teams in the state could be better than we were if we were going to win.

Over time I realized how many of those "perfect" circumstances were out of my control. Even if everything else fell into place, all it would take is for one single team to be better than we were, and then the goal of being state champions would be unattainable. After a time I came to the conclusion that we might not—and probably would not—ever win a state championship because of how many factors were involved.

That was a moment of personal reflection. If I was coaching for the main purpose of winning a state championship, then it probably was time to retire. I would most likely never achieve that purpose.

And then came my epiphany. As I thought about my purpose, I realized why I was really coaching. I knew how much the life lessons associated with running in high school and college had changed my life, and I discovered that my real reason for coaching was that I wanted to help make that same positive difference in young runners' lives that had happened in mine. More important than winning a state championship was what runners could learn about life through the process. I decided to keep coaching for that purpose, to lead young people to those life lessons.

Since that day when I decided that we would never win a state championship and that winning was not my main purpose for coaching, we have won six state championships.

I don't claim to be able to completely explain how that happened! But I do believe that it has a lot to do with identifying true purpose, concentrating on what is most important, and following it through to the end. That's why your first step must be to discover your own purpose, *the* reason you get up in the morning, and to be aware of that purpose starting the moment you slide out of bed and your feet first hit the floor.

What is your purpose?

What is the one thing that defines your day, drives your choices, and results in your fulfillment?

Most people don't know the answer to either of those questions. They confuse the answers with their daily agenda and their to-do list. A list of things to be done is not the same thing as your purpose. It took me time to realize that mine revolved around "making a difference" rather than "making runners faster."

Do you remember the movie *City Slickers* that starred Billy Crystal and Jack Palance? In it Billy's character Mitch Robbins, an ad executive in mid-life crisis, asks the wise old cowboy Curly about the meaning of life.

> Curly: "Do you know what the secret of Life is?"
>
> "What's that?" Mitch, the tenderfoot, prods.
>
> Curly: "One thing. And that's what you have to figure out for yourself."

It's time for *you* to figure out that one thing.

You *do* have a purpose even if you've never thought about it or defined it. When our children were younger, on a vacation in Florida we visited a bird sanctuary founded by a man called The Pelican Man. During our time there The Pelican Man was slowly walking around the area, and he was like a bird magnet. Rescued birds in cages called out to him, and small wild song birds from the area landed on his shoulders, often three of them perched there at one time. Clearly Pelican Man had found, and pursued, his purpose.

At lunch we talked about the amazing old man surrounded by birds and how powerful his purpose was. During the conversation I glanced at my eleven-year old daughter Megan and saw that a tear was rolling down her cheek. When asked what was wrong, Megan responded, "I'm just afraid that I'm never going to have a purpose."

No need to worry. Twenty years later she wakes up every day as a motivated, purposeful person. With thoughtful and active reflection you can too.

The act of discovering it is often a process. Earlier in my coaching career, I believed that my purpose was directly tied to how fast our runners could become. Then I had another moment of epiphany: as an adult, there isn't a whole lot of life benefit to being able to run fast! Maybe if you are a zookeeper, a beekeeper, or a NASCAR pit crew member, but otherwise there are a lot more important skills to learn. That is another time when I realized my purpose needed to be something beyond just getting teenagers to run fast or getting them to memorize soliloquies from *Hamlet*. My purpose should not be to see how many items I can get crossed out on a day's agenda.

What is your purpose? What one idea is going to become your focus in your every day search for excellence? Think about it, ponder it, mull it over.

You don't have to become frozen in marble like a Rodin sculpture to think about it. Just make a concerted effort to spend time while walking, or showering, or driving. Ask yourself probing questions:

"What do I devote the largest portion of my day to doing?"

"Is this the most important thing I do?"

"What people have been the most influential in my life?"

"What did they do to have such a strong impact on me?"

"What defining moments in my life have shaped who I have become?"

"What parts of my life are the most fulfilling?"

"If I could do only one thing today, what would I choose so that at the end of the day I would be proud?"

Come up with your answer. Test it out. Share it with someone you trust. Think about it some more. You'll find that this act will lead you to evaluate the ways in which you spend your time. It will make you question some of your decisions. It will clarify many of the gray areas in your life.

Here are some possible purposes, not meant to be a menu for you to choose from, but rather some examples:

Be a great mom.

Turn this business around.

Create something that lasts.

Be a positive role model.

Contribute.

Become more spiritual.

Lead.

Learn more.

Make a difference.

How do you know when you have chosen wisely? A purpose that becomes the focal point for you every day should bring "yes" answers to these three questions:

1. Does this purpose represent the person I want to be?
2. Is the fulfillment of this purpose within my control?
3. Will my commitment to this purpose lead me to go to bed satisfied and to wake up motivated to continue the journey?

A purpose that evokes three "Yes" answers looks to be a great fit for you. Embrace it, and feel good about looking yourself in the eye in the mirror.

Remember, this purpose may change as your life changes, as you age, and as you find yourself in new situations. Reviewing and reevaluating your purpose in these cases is healthy and allows you to continue to help yourself pay the most attention to what is most important.

Once you have your purpose, put it immediately into action. Write it down, and set it next to your alarm clock. Tape a copy to the mirror in your bathroom. Hang a laminated copy from your shower head. Slide a copy into your slippers. Your goal is to be aware of that purpose from the moment you wake up.

Author Garth Stein in his novel *The Art of Racing in the Rain* locks into this idea through a car racing metaphor. In the novel the main character, race car driver Denny, talks about being in the zone where the driver is completely focused on his car's path. "Your car goes where your eyes go," meaning your path will follow your vision whether you are looking at the obstacles or you are looking at your goal.

I remember that same thing happening when learning to ride a bicycle. At first, if there was a car parked anywhere on the street, even one fifty yards ahead, my bike would magically steer toward it as if being pulled by a huge magnet. I'd have to put my feet down and pull the front tire to the side to avoid hitting that car. Why did I veer from the safe path? Why was I drawn right to that obstacle? Eventually I realized that as I was riding, I looked ahead at that parked car instead of looking ahead on the road where I wanted to ride. Once I learned to concentrate on the path I wanted to take, the obstacles were easy to pass by. "Your car goes where your eyes go." Your eyes must be focused on your purpose.

When you wake up and are immediately aware of your purpose, your feet hit the floor differently. The shower is warmer, your clothes are neater, and the coffee smells bolder. Preparing for the day turns from mindless to meaningful. While your agenda and lists still play in your mind, checking things off is no longer your main intent. Your main goal is to apply yourself to your purpose.

A teacher colleague has chosen her purpose to be "Make a difference with every student every day." She was thoughtful in this choice, and she has trained herself to be cognizant of this purpose from the moment she wakes up in the morning. She says that a daily sense of her purpose has not only affected her class time, it has affected her awareness of many other circumstances that make a difference for the students. This teacher makes it a habit to spend a few minutes chatting positively with the office personnel before school because she has realized that those are the first people our students come in contact with, and she wants that opening interaction to be a good one. She has also recognized that her class period starts better if students are immediately engaged, so she stands at her doorway, smiles, and greets each one of them by name, which gets them interacting with her immediately.

She now connects more positively with parents, knowing how a teacher/parent relationship can impact the "difference with students" she is striving to make. She grades papers differently. She even has a different outlook on occasional student resistance. All these things have come, not from the curriculum, but from her focus on "making a difference with every student every day." As you might imagine, her positive influence has affected not only her students but our entire school.

What might this approach look like in your family? In your business?

What would the impact be? How would you feel about that impact?

When your purpose becomes a daily motivation, you become what I call a "seven sevenths person." Unfortunately, most people are "two sevenths" people, those who merely survive throughout the work week while holding on for the weekend. Again, the surrounding culture perpetuates this attitude. Ever have the radio playing at the same time each morning? This is what you hear throughout the week:

"We're sorry! It's Monday. Hang in there and get through it."

"Happy Wednesday, it's hump day! Getting over the hump and halfway to the weekend."

"Friday, Friday, Friday has finally arrived! Survive one more day and the weekend is here!"

As a result of constant feedback like that, and because they may not even be aware of their lack of clear purpose, many people waste five-sevenths of their lives (weekdays) while waiting for the other two-sevenths (weekends). How will your life change when you begin to live for your purpose every day?

A few years ago in a literature class I was teaching, a student sage made a remark that tied attitude into philosophy. Students were engaged in a Socratic seminar where they were discussing the idea of "purpose" as it applied to the priest, a main character in *The Power and the Glory*. In the midst of the discussion Sam stood up at his desk, held his hands out wide, and said, "I've got it! Here is how you define 'purpose.' If you are a window washer, do you see your purpose as cleaning windows...or do you see your purpose as helping other people see clearly?"

There was silence in the room. Sam not only understood purpose but was able to put the idea into an analogy for the rest of the class. Are you washing windows OR are you helping others see clearly?

The same lesson came to a girl who worked on a church mission trip where she and her friends were asked to sand the drywall inside a house so that it could be painted. For three days they applied themselves to this tedious task. Long days of scraping and sweating. Each morning they had trouble even finding the spot where they had stopped the night before.

Tired and bored, the girl was griping to her mission-mates one evening at dinner. Unbeknownst to her, the director of the program was nearby and overheard the complaints. He walked up to where she was sitting, made eye contact with her, and gently said, "You're not just sanding drywall. You're turning a house into a home."

Or you're helping other people see clearly. Or you're building a cathedral. See the pattern?

No matter how it's phrased, this is another great lesson in getting the right perspective on your purpose. Know it, then pursue it. One of the most significant lessons I've learned about pursuing purpose every day came several years ago. It was on a snowy February day, one where the meteorologists predicted a dusting and then were surprised by a seven inch snowfall overnight. Because our town's plows couldn't work fast enough in the wet snow, my family woke up to an unexpected "snow day," a day off from school.

Snow days are a little glimpse of heaven. A teacher's mind which is so focused on the day's lessons all of a sudden becomes clear and peaceful. Nothing really has to be done. That February morning my wife and children went back to bed. I sat with my feet propped up on the couch, hot cup of cocoa by my side, with the television—and remote control!—all to myself. Just as I was settling in, the phone rang. It was 8:00 am.

I groused to myself about my relaxing moment being disturbed. When I picked up the receiver, a male voice spoke. He didn't say "hi," he didn't identify himself, he just said this:

"Coach, it's a great day to get better. Now, how are we going to do it?"

I recognized the voice immediately. It was one of our senior distance runners named Ryan. He knew that we had scheduled a hard track workout that day, and he knew that the snow was a huge obstacle. Most importantly, he knew that this workout could be a key ingredient in his training, and he knew that, as a senior, he didn't have a lot of time left. In his mind, with his strong sense of purpose, he couldn't miss this workout. "It's a great day to get better. Now, how are we going to do it?"

I admit to being a little ashamed at that moment. While I was settling in comfortably for a "free" day, Ryan had his purpose fully in mind. While I was looking for a day off, even at 8:00 in the morning Ryan was thinking about how to fulfill his purpose of being the best runner he could be in the time that he had left in high school. How motivating that purpose had become for him!

The end of this story with Ryan is a good one. That afternoon we organized runners who shoveled and cleared lanes on our track so he (and they) could run the workout. Continuing to show the commitment to his purpose and the work ethic that it takes, Ryan went on to run a personal best time in the State Track Finals and then to compete in college. As you might expect, today he is the successful director of a non-profit organization, and he continues to wake up each day with an understanding of his purpose.

The conclusion of that story for me is that I ended up being a better coach, a better teacher, and a better person because of that phone call. I learned a lot about the power and inspiration behind a sense of purpose and how that applies to seeking excellence. I keep Ryan's quote on a piece of paper taped above my computer at work: "It's a great day to get better. Now, how are we going to do it?"

Every day excellence begins with a clear purpose, one that enters the mind as soon as you are awake. That purpose is the road map, the GPS system, the pilot that steers your daily journey.

Find that purpose now! Make it a habit to wake up with it in mind. Enjoy the accomplishment that comes from following it.

Chapter 5: Show up with an Attitude

Do you have your purpose in mind?

On my journey as an educator, this daily purpose works for me: Teach every student, every class period, every day.

Our cross-country team functions according to these statements of purpose:

1. Hard work, given time, will beat talent.
2. Every day is a great day to get better. (Thanks, Ryan!)
3. To seek excellence, you must become an every day person.

One challenge is that these thoughts are merely words unless we become dedicated in our efforts to develop an attitude that supports the pursuit of our purpose, especially in light of the negativity that surrounds us.

It's almost a cliche to hear that you must have a "positive attitude." It conjures up images of the big yellow smiley face often found on tee shirts and bumper stickers. That doesn't seem to be very practical.

Many times the phrase "positive attitude" is not defined clearly which often leads to misunderstanding and unrealistic approaches to applying a nebulous concept of positive attitude to specific daily challenges.

For clarity in our discussion, here is the definition we will use:

Positive attitude: an outlook in which you don't allow any one person or any one thing make you negative for very long.

The emphasis in that definition is the phrase "for very long." The definition is not suggesting that you can adopt an attitude where you will never be angry, upset, sad, or negative. It is not promoting denial since it is unrealistic to believe that a positive attitude will keep you from ever becoming negative. Life often has painful challenges, and it's healthy to acknowledge that fact and know that some events will occur that provoke negative thoughts.

But we want to avoid being like those students who, because of one bad bowl of cereal, have decided that they are having a "terrible day." The secret is to stop the nagging occurrences in life from keeping us negative for very long. The line at the grocery is moving slowly: don't let that affect the rest of your day. The cable TV goes out during your favorite show: deal with it and read a book. Your brand new car gets a scratch in the parking lot: take a *really* deep breath, or maybe two or three, and stay positive about the rest of your day.

Kyle Burton, a student and runner, found this definition of positive attitude to be so valuable that he created and added to it a "Fifteen Minute Rule." When something difficult happens during his day, Kyle allows himself fifteen minutes of negativity, and then he moves on with his positive attitude (and with his journey toward excellence). He often checks his wristwatch to see how many of his negative minutes he has left. Recently, he has added an amendment to the rule. Kyle actually counts his negative thoughts during that fifteen minute time period, and he makes himself come up with twice as many positive thoughts afterwards. These positive thoughts often begin with "One thing I learned from this was..." What a great way to monitor a daily positive attitude! What a great way to regain focus on his purpose!

Once you recognize the challenges that surround you, you can work to make your own set of structures that keep you accountable to that positive attitude because it's what will support you through the events that inevitably distract you or tempt you away from your purpose. One structure that has worked for runners on our team is that we hold each other accountable for eliminating the phrase "have to" when we speak. The premise behind this is that there are very few things that we *have* to do. Very few things in our lives are mandated. Most things are those we *choose* to do or, better yet, *get* to do.

When runners ask about practice, the coaches have trained them not to say, "What do we *have to* run today?" Wording the question that way suggests that they are being forced to train, when actually they need to embrace the opportunity to run because that is how they will improve. Instead, the coaches have runners ask, "What do we *get to* run today?" Just changing that phrasing contributes to the positive feeling of embracing and doing what is necessary to improve every day as a runner.

This upbeat phrasing becomes so ingrained in the runners that it often carries over to other areas of their lives. A fellow English teacher once said that one of our runners asked in class, "When we finish this novel, do we get to write a paper?" I've had a mother brag about her son at home after dinner asking, "Which one of us gets to do the dishes?"

What a healthy way to approach the tasks in our lives, the thought that we get to do them rather than have to do them. How might a daily "get to" approach affect your world?

"What is the first project I get to do at work today?"

"How many diapers will I get to change this morning?"

"What will I get to learn in class this period?"

"Do I get to take a bath?"

This concept finds its roots in Mark Twain's iconic character Tom Sawyer. Remember when Tom was told to whitewash the fence while all his friends were off fishing and having fun? Tom chose to make the chore a "get to" task, one that looked to be so much fun that eventually his friends gave him gifts so that they could do his work for him. This "get to" attitude keeps situations from being negative for very long.

Just being aware of our surroundings can also help the positive momentum. One of my first bosses always said, "There will be a crisis every day. Some big, some small, but there will always be a crisis." While that initially sounds despairing, it actually helps when you can anticipate and accept the challenges and obstacles that occur. By anticipating these, you can have a Plan B ready if or when your Plan A falls apart. People who strive to seek excellence every day know that they often have to count on the quality of their Plan Bs.

Author Richard Bach put it this way in his novel *Illusions*: "You are never given a problem without a gift for you in its hands. We seek problems because we need their gifts." When we are tired, when we are disappointed, when we feel overwhelming challenges, this is when we call upon our purpose and attitude for our unshakeable foundation. This is when need all the benefits that come from being positive.

Profound understanding of the power of the proper attitude was evident in a conversation I had with Bob Sutherland, the owner of a store in Northern Michigan called "Cherry Republic," a store that takes advantage of the state's bounteous crop to sell all things cherry: salsa, granola, coffee, pie, wine, condiments, and my favorite dark chocolate covered cherries. The company employs the most genuinely positive people I have ever come in contact with. They are not the "Have a nice day" required-to-act-happy people many businesses employ; the Cherry Republic employees sincerely enjoy being at work every day. My sister Anne once called their business with a shipping problem, and when she hung up the phone, she said, "I feel like I just made that woman's day because I had a problem she could solve!"

I once had the opportunity to meet Bob the boss, and so I straightforwardly asked him, "What have you done to create that incredibly positive atmosphere?"

Here was his reply: "When our business first began to expand and I knew we needed summer help for the tourist season, I went to the local high school and asked for the names of their fifteen best students. I wrote personal letters to all fifteen students, inviting them to come work for me. Eight of those students came to work, and at the end of the summer, do you know what I discovered? Those were not the right students for me to employ."

I was surprised, not at all what I expected his conclusion to be. Bob continued, "So the next spring when I was ready to hire summer employees, I went back to the high school and asked for the names of the fifteen students that teachers most liked to see walk into their classrooms, students who were upbeat, enthusiastic, energetic, and eager to learn. I wrote *those* students personal letters, eight of them came to work for me, and from that moment the atmosphere at our store was great.

Those positive young people had an effect on every one of our employees, no matter what age. Our business has been booming ever since."

Cherry Republic has flourished with that combination of philosophy and attitude.

Remember that negative culture discussed in chapter two, the one that surrounds us and picks away at our resolve? Author Garth Stein's car racing metaphor for this continues: "A man who drives a two-thousand-pound car at one hundred seventy miles per hour does not get flustered by the honking of the geese." Ignore the honking. Ignore the geese. Ignore the negative.

I find myself noticing examples of the right attitude all around me. One of the simplest recently occurred as a boy and a girl were walking together toward my classroom door. The girl, one of my students, said good-bye to the boy, and here is what he said to her in return: "Go get your education."

Exactly. Know your purpose, and train your attitude to support that purpose. Now you're on the way to finding excellence in your life every day.

Chapter 6: Finish up with a Flourish

"TGIF--Thank God It's Friday" is seldom uttered because the speaker is happy to still have one more workday to get things done. "TGIF" has come into common usage by people who are surviving the work week while waiting for the weekend. Why is it so hard to be a "seven sevenths" person? Why do so many people begin coasting as the weekend nears? People get tired, and without a strong philosophical focus and the attitude to support it, their pursuit of excellence just disappears.

The culture which surrounds us is often one where people waste the end of one time period as they anticipate the beginning of the next one. This is never more apparent than in every high school in May. Seniors come down with "senioritis," a self-inflicted disease, and they quickly begin to go through the motions of the school day rather than getting quality learning out of their time. Often a senior will put a countdown number of days on his locker, tearing one off as each day begins. Phone apps and online countdowns and alarms exist that make senioritis even more lethal! That countdown makes the end of school drag on interminably as the focus becomes just getting the year over with.

This TGIF, or for seniors TGITEOMHSC (ThankGodIt'sTheEndOfMyHighSchoolCareer,) attitude is certainly not limited to eighteen year olds who are eager for their diplomas. It permeates the world around us. One day as I stood in the check-out line at a retail store, the cashier was having trouble accessing a coupon that the woman in line in front of me was using. The cashier tried to scan it once, then twice, then a third time, no use. Needing a register key, she called for help over the store's PA system. We waited for several minutes. People in line began rolling their eyes at each other. The cashier again called for help. Several more minutes went by. Finally, the cashier looked over to the staff break area where a woman with a manager's tag was sitting. The cashier called to her for help.

Not twenty feet away from where our line had been paralyzed for ten minutes, that manager called back to the cashier, "Get someone else. I'm not on the clock."

We waited a few more minutes, and finally the cashier walked over to talk to the manager quietly. The manager reluctantly shuffled over to our line, emitted a big sigh, pulled out her key, and opened the register. The coupon was scanned. The line began to move. The whole process took the manager fewer than thirty seconds. "I'm not on the clock" is never heard from someone with strong sense of purpose.

Sometimes TGIF manifests itself in a more comical way. One Friday afternoon at school all the teachers received an email from the school nurse, an email that must have been on her to-do list all week, and she was scrambling to get it checked off before the weekend. When opened, the email read, "Attached is a list of signs and symptoms of an impending stroke. Have a nice weekend." For some reason the timing of that message felt a little off!

"I'm not on the clock."

"TGIF."

You can't afford to be like these people. The nearer you get to the end of one time period, the more you must keep your purpose in mind and support it with your positive attitude. It's sustaining your efforts. You can be distinctively different. You can learn to finish up with a flourish.

Take pride in being a "seven sevenths" person. Fight back against TGIF! I am revealing a big secret here, but at our school when a second-semester senior puts a daily countdown list on his locker, someone tapes up a piece of paper beneath it that says, "Don't count the days; make the days count." Each day that the senior removes that unsolicited advice from under his calendar, someone tapes the same message up again. As you might have guessed, that "someone" who tapes up the make-the-days-count message is me. And I can be very persistent in my attempts to get the message through to balance the TGIF-like message of the countdown.

I heard a similar philosophy to "finish with a flourish" many years ago when I had watched a musical performance on a cruise ship. The morning after that show I happened to run into one of the singers, and I told her how impressed I was that she could perform with such energy in spite of the fact that she was singing the same songs three shows a night, six nights a week. "How are you able to summon such enthusiasm?" I asked.

Her answer gave me a lot to think about: "I always remember that no matter how many times I have played the same show, the people in the audience are seeing it for the very first time.

I want them to experience the show with the excitement of that first-time feeling."

I've used this example in working with teachers who have taught the same lesson five times in one day and are getting ready to teach it one more time. "Remember that these students are hearing it for their first time. Give them the first-time energy." With this idea in mind, the end of the day can be just as productive as the beginning; Friday can be just as productive as Monday.

Have you ever seen a track race where a runner thinks he has a race won, so he coasts the final meters to the finish line? Carl Lewis, one of America's greatest Olympians, once celebrated a victory in the 200 meter dash by raising both arms and coasting the final twenty meters. He won the race but missed the world record by .03 seconds. Though his career lasted ten more years, he never broke that record.

More recently a video has gone viral of a steeplechaser from the University of Oregon who celebrates with the crowd because of his big lead in the finishing stretch. Unfortunately, the celebration proves premature as another runner sprints by him right at the finish line. Just a month later at Atlanta's prestigious Peachtree 10K Road Race, professional Ben Payne, excited to be winning a race featuring 60,000 runners, raised the "I'm number one!" finger to the crowd and coasted the last few meters to the finish. One step before the line, fellow competitor Scott Overall appeared at his side and leaned his body ahead to win the race, proving it's not enough to be ahead at meter 9,999 in a 10,000 meter race.

"Run hard to the very end" beats "TGIF" every time!

A veteran teacher named Carl Wagner has not only embraced the finishing flourish in his own life, he has taught it to his students who have embraced it also. He began thinking about the idea because of "casual Friday," a more and more commonly accepted practice in the education and business worlds. Carl's observation was that the act of turning Friday, 20% of the work week, into a casual day, one where teachers are allowed (and sometimes encouraged) to "dress down," greatly lessens production from students and workers. "Casual" often sends the subtle message that the school/business expects a lower level of effort and commitment that day.

One Friday a student came into Carl's class and announced, "Please tell me we're not going to do any work today. We should be rewarded for a good week." Always aware of "teachable moments," Carl seized that opportunity and created a special mini-lesson that day and each remaining Friday called "MOE: moment of excellence" where his classes view inspirational videos and discuss quotes from successful people in all areas of life, from opera to small business to parenting to music to athletics to classical art. He alternates the Friday lessons: one week he presents notes and ideas about excellence and the next week a student brings in and presents a specific example.

Carl's selling point is that someone who makes the most of Fridays will always achieve at a higher level than someone who is coasting. Friday is the greatest opportunity to separate yourself from other people. If you make Fridays just as valuable as the other days of the week, people will sense something different about you, something that would set you apart from others that might be competing with you for a job. That message is powerful for students: be aware of what others are like and be distinctly different. Carl's students responded by making Fridays their most productive day of the week.

How positive an impact will that have on their college experience? How valuable will that make them as employees? How would the world change if the mantra for the fifth day of the work week stopped being "TGIF" and started being "MOE"?

Keeping one's focus on purpose, not just every day of the week but also over a long period of time, can lead to especially significant achievements. Several years ago I had the opportunity to spend about thirty minutes with Al Oerter, one of the most accomplished United States Olympians ever, having won the discus in four successive Olympic Games, 1956-1960-1964-1968, and demonstrating excellence at the highest level for over twenty years. He was very patient with me as I peppered him with questions and took notes on all his answers. One powerful thing he said was this, "Goals that take a long time to achieve are much more satisfying than those that are achieved quickly. Everyone wants the quick path to achievement. I am a testament to the fact that long-term accomplishments are much more personally fulfilling."

Oerter's statement and his four Olympic gold medals seem to directly contrast some of the current culture's infatuation with "quick wins." Patience for results is in short supply. Young athletes often try a sport and want to be good immediately. If not, they give up and move on to something else. Employees covet promotions and raises without wanting to demonstrate corporate commitment. Many investors are scammed in get-rich-quick schemes because of their unwillingness to see a long-term picture. Al Oerter, by word and by accomplishment, demonstrates both the achievement of excellence and the every day, day after day, year after year, approach.

How do we gain the patience we need? What short-term satisfaction can occur while we are focused on long term achievement? How do we find joy in the journey?

The answer is to learn to appreciate the process, to find something good in every day. One outlook is to realize that every day, no matter how good or how bad, will always have a best moment. Every week will always have a best moment. Every task will always have a best moment. That's why we need Fridays. That's why we need to become seven-sevenths people.

Several years ago we had a senior runner named Tim who was a very thoughtful and philosophical young man. Most of his conversations with me started with him saying, "Coach, I've been thinking…"

That's how it started one afternoon. "Coach, I've been thinking…"

"Yes, Tim?" (What now?)

"I've been thinking a lot about upcoming graduation for us seniors. The senior classes before us have each left a legacy on our team:

state championships, work ethic, positive attitude, and team spirit. I'm concerned that we will graduate not having left anything as our legacy."

I told you he was philosophical. An eighteen year old Socrates. Although he was part of a group of young men who would win three consecutive state championships, obviously this wasn't enough "legacy" for Tim. I asked him this: "What has your group of seniors done that has been significant?"

"That's just it," he sighed. "We haven't done anything special. All we've done is just show up every day and run."

Show up *every day* and run. Can you imagine any greater legacy? Tim didn't see it as anything special, but I contend that very few people in life "show up" every day and "run." Very few people bring their best efforts every day to what is most important to them. People make excuses, take days off, coast on Fridays, and sometimes are just too preoccupied. Actually, Tim and his fellow seniors may have established the best legacy of all.

Show up every day and run.

Chapter 7: Finding the gem stone

Many of you reading this book are in a leadership role with younger people; you may be a parent, care giver, teacher, coach, advisor, counselor, or mentor. Others of you are in roles where you work with or supervise adults in various capacities. One of the questions I am most frequently asked is "How do I help the other people I'm around develop purpose and the right attitude?"

There are two basic principles that may help you apply the first six chapters to people you work with or who are under your guidance.

Basic Principle 1: Most people, including teenagers, want to be motivated.

Basic Principle 2: Most people don't know how to be self-motivated.

People want to be motivated so that they can create for themselves a brighter future. Young people know they will be competing with peers for class rankings, for spots in prestigious universities, and for fulfilling careers. Older people know they will be competing for job opportunities. But most just aren't sure what to do first. They don't have a plan. They need knowledge and encouragement.

This is where you come in. The same steps that you've been reading about (Wake up with a purpose, Show up with an attitude, Finish up with a flourish) will work for them. However, these concepts are often very foreign to people.

This may be especially true with teenagers. As negative as the culture is around adults, multiply that to see what teens must overcome. They are surrounded by unmotivated peers (not their fault) and they are quick to want to blend in with that crowd.

Your guidance and one-to-one attention can show them that there is another way. Again, I promise you that you will be surprised how many people will respond to someone offering them a more positive direction.

When working with others, be patient. Define all terms. Break all steps into smaller ones. For example, as you help someone understand their purpose, you may need to give models to help them see what this should look like. Then help them break theirs down into meaningful, achievable parts. Give them ownership in what they choose, but give them structure in how to proceed.

Suppose you are working with a teenager who says she wants her statement of purpose to be:

"To do my best in everything."

While a powerful and valid statement, its abstractness makes it difficult to achieve. So you ask qualifying questions.

What is the major area in which you want to do your best each day?

What must your effort level be for you to achieve this?

How will you remind yourself of this purpose during the day?

What will be your measure at the end of the day that you have done your best?

Just as you are doing personally, stress the idea that every day excellence is a process, and think about ways to recognize or reward the positive strides they take on this journey. On our cross country team we encourage our runners to apply themselves daily to improve (reminder from chapter 5: To seek excellence, you must become an every day person). To acknowledge their efforts and to reward the process, our runners who run 100 days in a row earn a pencil, just a normal wooden pencil engraved with the words "I am an every day person!" For the coach a pencil is a ten cent investment; for the runners those pencils become invaluable, prized possessions because of the effort that goes into earning them and because of the recognition they receive for that effort.

Teaching them to apply themselves to a goal on a daily basis gives these young people one of the greatest gifts you can give them. How successful will they be as college students! How great will they be as employees! How strong will they be as parents! How motivating will they be to the other people in their lives!

Can you see how this applies to your children? To your friends and colleagues? To your employees?

Ignore stereotypes. Some people you might expect to be motivated are not. Many you might never expect to be motivated are dying for someone to show them the way, to give them an opportunity, and to believe in them, sometimes even more than they believe in themselves.

An apt analogy for this idea of not being fooled by stereotypes and for the rest of the process of working with people has to do with the polishing of petoskey stones.

You may not be aware of this fact, but many states have a "state stone" and Michigan's is the petoskey stone. Since I was little, our family has vacationed in the summer near the shores of Lake Michigan, and petoskeys have always been a part of that experience. These stones, hexagonal fossils that have fused together in rock-like form, are found on the shoreline of Lake Michigan. As stones, petoskeys appear gray and ordinary; when polished, they become beautiful, valuable stones that are used in rings, bracelets, and earrings.

Someone "hunts" petoskeys by walking slowly along the edge of the lake, looking carefully through the myriad stones that are washed up to shore with each wave. The challenge to finding them is twofold: 1) they are usually mixed in with many other types of stones, and 2) if a petoskey is dry, the coral-shaped fossil pattern is only faintly visible. To be a petoskey hunter, you must be a patient and discerning observer. You often have to sift through large piles of rocks to find just one petoskey. In dry sand you may often have to wet a stone or two in order to find the coral fossil pattern.

I remember learning about this process as a boy. While on vacation some days our family would go to the Lake Michigan beach. My mom and my sister would read books while I would play in the water and build things in the sand. My dad would walk along the shoreline. Very slowly. I could see him off in the distance, looking down, occasionally picking something up. Sometimes he would throw it out into the lake. Other times he would put it in the plastic pail he was carrying. My dad was hunting—and finding—petoskey stones.

I wanted to find them, too. So I would sprint down to my dad, kicking up the spray of the water as I ran, desperate to see a petoskey. I was terrible at finding them. One time I whined to my father, "Why can't I ever find one when you find so many?"

"Move your right foot," Dad said. "You're standing on one." He was correct. The search takes patience and concentration.

Once you have found a petoskey, you have an identifiable Michigan souvenir. If you want to increase its value, you "polish" it, often through a time-intensive effort by hand. Many layers have built up on top of the stone over thousands of years. Your job as polisher is to scrape those layers off to uncover the stone's true beauty. Beginning with a heavy grade of sandpaper, you scrape the stone and rinse off the debris, then again scrape and rinse the stone. Switching to a lighter sandpaper grade, you scrape and rinse over and over. Finally after progressing to the lightest grade, the coral patterns on the stone are distinct and vivid. You then apply a light polish to preserve your work, and this formerly nondescript, gray rock has been transformed into a beautiful gem.

You can see the parts of this analogy, comparing polishing a petoskey to your work with other people. Underscore these main points:

> Finding those who want to be motivated takes patience, but they can be found in the crowd.

> They may appear ordinary at first, but the valuable stone is under those layers.

> It takes time and effort for you to polish them, often needing more involvement at first (heavier grade sandpaper) and then lightening up as the process proceeds.

The end result is often more than anyone else expected. You recognized the potential when others didn't.

One figurative case of that polishing progression that immediately comes to mind is Trevor, a young man who earned Ds in freshman English. His natural intelligence was enough for him to do better, but his immaturity and lack of proper study habits overwhelmed him. However, over time, his journey as a student became a day to day process, and gradually as he grew older, he developed greater intellectual curiosity. To supplement that, he slowly increased his work ethic, and by the end of his senior year, Trevor received a 5 on his AP English test.

From a gray stone to a gem stone. Sometimes several mentors are working together at polishing, and sometimes those gray-stone people develop the skills to polish themselves. That might be stretching the analogy a little bit, but it sure is exciting when it happens.

This same progression happened with a runner named Jessica. Conscientious from the beginning of her career, she finished 122nd in the state cross-country finals as a freshman. Her journey accelerated because of what she learned along the way about training, nutrition, and recovery. Jessica's sophomore year she improved to 64th in the state, and she became even more motivated to pursue running excellence in some way every day. What a valuable "petoskey" Jessica became: 9th in the state as a junior and 6th as a senior. Every teacher, coach, and mentor of hers was part of the polishing process, and Jessica herself became a huge contributor.

Sometimes those you work with haven't reached their final shine by the time they leave you and move on. How many parents know this! You lay the best foundation you can, and then time and real life experiences combine to finish the process. Sometimes your work on the petoskey doesn't show itself until much later. That's why you must keep your faith in the polishing process and the impact you are having.

Yes, working with others is a lot like finding and polishing petoskeys. But this analogy is also a good reminder of our own journey toward excellence. There are some days where I don't feel any more valuable than that gray stone. There are some days where the sandpaper that is scraping against me is made up of challenges, troubles, disappointments, pain, and grief, but all those things are really part of the every day process, polishing me and who I am becoming. We must understand and remember that the sandpaper challenges of life are polishing us, and we must learn to see the value in our daily efforts.

There is great fulfillment in becoming an every day person seeking excellence in your own life, but there may be even more satisfaction in mentoring those around you to understand and own this process. What a gift you have given them, one that will keep on giving to them the rest of their lives.

Chapter 8: Responding realistically

As mentioned earlier when discussing positive attitude, it would be unhealthy to pretend that life doesn't present some heavy duty challenges, ones that have an impact far beyond the reach of Kyle's 15 minute rule. Remember, just as it's unrealistic to expect your positive attitude to mean you will never feel negative, it would also be unrealistic not to spend some words here acknowledging that some truly tragic events can, and do, occur.

Death, job loss, divorce, broken relationships, and spiritual hollowness fit into this category, and certainly you can name others. These events bring pain and grief, emptiness, confusion, temporary depression, and often great introspection.

While the Purpose-Positive attitude-Finishing flourish approach can make a significant impact daily, and while it can be a help in life's most challenging times, it is not a "cure" for the grief that we sometimes face. This approach is meant to help us make the most of each day; it's not meant to be a panacea.

Over the years as a quick bit of personal motivation, I have trained myself to answer "Great!" whenever someone asks me, "How're you doing?" Saying it reminds me to feel great, and it makes me feel stronger and better especially on challenging days. I had grown to answer "Great" subconsciously through the years, so I was surprised by my own word at my father's funeral.

At the funeral when people asked, "How are you?" it was no longer a meaningless bit of conversation. So I had to consciously choose to answer with "Not great" or "Not great but it will get better." I share that story with you to be sure that you recognize that life will present some really tough times. What you've read here and put into practice will help during those times, but it will not whitewash them.

It's also good to recognize and keep perspective on your purpose. Lately, as a teacher/coach/mentor, I've been waking up to this thought: Make a difference every day. This has worked really well for me as I come into contact with students, athletes, and colleagues. Recently on a Saturday my wife Amy and I were travelling by car on a trip that would take all day. When I awoke with the thought about making a difference, I first wondered how I was going to be able to do that since I wouldn't be at school. Fortunately, Perspective spoke to me and said, "Wait a minute! Making a difference means making a difference! This is a great opportunity for you to have an impact on Amy's day, to make it positive and fulfilling for her." I felt chagrined. Of course that should be my motivation for the day. Sometimes we need practical perspective to remind us of the scope of what we have pledged to do.

Sometimes, we have days where our purpose becomes a lot simpler. My friend Phil tells a story about a time he was trout fishing in a remote stream in northern Colorado. He had started in the morning when it was cool, but as the day heated up, he removed his jacket and was left casting in just an old fraternity tee shirt, raggedy shorts, a broken-billed hat, and his waders. Phil's frustration built throughout the day as he just couldn't catch anything. He kept casting and reeling, casting and reeling, to no avail. No fish. Much frustration.

In the late afternoon another fisherman arrived and waded into the stream near where Phil was standing. They exchanged greetings, and the second fisherman recognized the fraternity logo on Phil's shirt. Having been a member of that same fraternity but at a different college, the second fisherman remembered how members of that national fraternity would formally greet one another in brotherhood.

He spoke the secret, mystical fraternal words to Phil. "What is your purpose?"

The day of frustration overrode any fraternal recognition Phil had at that time. He rolled his eyes and answered honestly, "I'm just trying to catch a stupid fish!"

There are days when your purpose won't feel very noble. Tragedies will challenge it, and sometimes "every day" becomes "everyday." There may even be a few days where you would be happy just to catch one stupid fish.

In times like these return as quickly as you can to the foundation: being mindful of your every day purpose and the attitude you have created to support it.

It may take time and effort, but you'll catch a lot more fish that way.

Chapter 9: Eight minutes of compassion

"To lead others, you must first lead yourself." That adage holds true as you are planning a specific purpose and attitude that will be the foundation of your daily activities. However, I would be remiss as an English teacher if I didn't add a quote from the poet John Donne: "No man is an island entire of himself."

The more positive and focused you become in your life, the more you will want to surround yourself with others like you. "Positive people make people positive" (my wife Amy's quote). Being aware of the culture around you will also make you more aware than ever of the type of people you spend your time with. The older I get, the more I appreciate spending time with upbeat, energetic people. When interviewing potential English teachers, I look for optimism and energy, people who will bring those qualities to the classroom, to our department, and to our school. In most instances and most circumstances, a positive attitude is contagious.

This also means that the responsibility falls on us to share that positivity with others, not only with those we love, those we work with, and those we see daily, but also with all the other people we come into contact with, no matter how short that contact time is. Compassion must also be part of this journey.

The word "compassion" itself can be made by combining "compass" and "passion." That's not what the ancient Greeks had in mind when they created the word; it's probably just a coincidence in the jumble of English letters. But looking at compassion that way blends well with our idea of purpose.

Compass: specific direction.

Passion: with energy and enthusiasm.

Another of Rick's definitions:

Compassion: Energy and enthusiasm applied in a specific direction.

How do we include compassion as a part of every day purpose? How do we use compassion to support both ourselves and others?

One way is to recognize opportunities to make a difference no matter how big or how small. One day Chris and Sloane, two of my students, hurried excitedly up to where I was doing hall duty. "Mr. Weinheimer, Mr. Weinheimer," they bubbled, "we have to tell you what happened last night when we got tired of studying and decided to order a pizza."

They had my attention.

"We ordered the pizza online, and at the end of the order form was a box that said, 'Special requests.' Since we had already filled in the kind of pizza we wanted, we had no idea what special requests would be. We were tired and feeling silly, so we typed into that box, 'Dragons vs. Unicorns, please.' We were laughing as we pushed the 'send order' button."

"Half an hour later, the pizza was delivered, and we were slightly disappointed that the delivery guy didn't say anything about our 'special request.' It was just the normal pizza transaction. But when we opened up the box to eat, we saw the inside of the lid. There, drawn on the cardboard in red and black marker, was the depiction of a huge, fire-breathing dragon glaring down at a bold, defiant unicorn!"

Does that fit the idea of compassion? Sure it does! Someone took five minutes and will never know how happy he made those kids. An act of compassion from a pizza chef with a Sharpie.

What "pizza chef/Sharpie" opportune moments occur during your typical day? Even if you can't draw a unicorn, can you sing, make a witty remark, laugh, smile, or listen to someone? How many chances do we have over the course of a day to bring positive energy to others? What an impact we will make if we take advantage of those opportunities, the Pizza Chef Compassion moments.

Compassion manifests itself in other ways. When our oldest son David was a freshman in high school, he thought he would enjoy theater and drama, so he auditioned for the fall play. Like most freshmen, he was cast in the ensemble. The lead role went to a boisterous, extroverted senior named Ben, the one who always got the lead because of his experience and his expertise. As the whole cast did, David spent many evenings at rehearsals, working at his small part to contribute to the whole effort. At a break during one practice the final week before the show, David found himself standing alone for a moment, and Ben walked up to speak to him. After a sentence or two of small talk, Ben said to David, "I've been watching, and you've worked hard for this show. I think you have a really good future in theater." David beamed.

How much that one sentence meant, uttered from an older, cooler senior lead to a freshman ensemble member. You never know how much impact a small act of compassion, like Ben's, can mean to someone. This is You can Be the Lead Someday compassion. By the way, our son David, now grown up, is a professional actor in New York City.

Compassion: energy and enthusiasm applied in a positive direction.

Another example of compassion revealed in a small moment: two years ago on our cross country team we had one of the fastest female runners in the country. One day while we were preparing to run a fast 2-mile on the track for our workout, I asked Mackenzie if she would rather run with the boys instead of the girls that day because the boys could push her to run a faster time. Mackenzie thought about that for a moment, shook her head no, and said, "Maybe that would help *me* get a faster time...but if I run with the girls, maybe I can set a fast pace that will help *all of them* get a faster time." Focus, purpose, and leadership. Setting the Pace for Others compassion.

I have had the opportunity to be the guest speaker several times at the sports' awards ceremony at Southside, a local elementary school. One of the most impressive examples of focus comes from them because they always send their school mission statement for me to connect my presentation to. One of their key words is "kindness," a great unifying word for a student body and one that the teachers attempt to tie into their lessons every day.

This past winter I again spoke to the students and parents of Southside, centering on the idea of kindness as it related to a recent tragic event that had occurred in our town. Josh, a highly successful, highly popular, highly respected senior basketball player had sustained life-threatening injuries in a car accident. In the weeks that followed, our school experienced the thoughtfulness, kindness, and compassion of coaches, teams, and student bodies from all over our state. One team warmed up in tee shirts with Josh's last name emblazoned on them. Another team took up a collection at their school to help defray medical expenses. Our rival school from across town showed up for a game and sat behind our team's bench, even standing during our school song as a sign of support.

This continued for many weeks, the We're in this Together type of compassion.

We are happy that Josh is now making a tremendous recovery, and we are thankful for the lessons about compassion that we all learned through the experience.

Perhaps the most powerful act of compassion I've witnessed personally came on a Sunday in late April of 2012. I was sitting on a plastic chair next to my mother in a semi-darkened room in the intensive care unit of a hospital. We were chatting quietly and watching as a ventilator controlled my father's breathing. My sister Anne and her husband Jeff had been in the room but stepped out for a moment. Suddenly, a machine began beeping. A nurse walked in, smiled at us, and said, "Let me take a look at those tubes." A moment later she added cheerfully, "Let me see if one of those needs to be changed."

The nurse worked patiently for a moment, but then a more serious expression came over her face. She began to work more frantically. At the same time she must have activated some kind of signal because suddenly two other nurses and a doctor rushed in. I realized what was happening, and with my heart in my throat, I sent a text message to Anne saying, "Come quickly."

The doctor on call that day in intensive care was a stranger to us. She looked at Dad, had terse conversation with the nurses, and then turned to Mom and me. "I'll give him some medicine," she said, "but I don't think it's going to help." Then after giving him a dose she added, "I can give him some more, but it won't help."

At that moment I knew we were losing Dad, and when I looked into that doctor's eyes, I could clearly see those eyes saying, "I'm sorry that I can't save him for you. I'm really sorry that I can't save him for you." Moments later, Dad's spirit was gone, and I called Amy to tell her.

The incredible compassion in that doctor's eyes stayed with me. The next day I looked at my phone and saw that I texted my sister at 1:43 and called my wife at 1:51. Eight minutes.

I had never seen that doctor before that moment, and I will never see her again. I don't even know her name. But her life intersected with mine for eight minutes of one of the most significant times I will ever experience. And I will carry that memory of the sincere compassion in her eyes forever. What a gift she gave me. Heartfelt Human compassion.

While we are looking to surround ourselves with positive people, we must be committed to act as compassionate people for others as well. Sincere compassion should be a significant piece of everyone's journey toward excellence. We can make a difference even in just eight minutes.

Compassion. Every day.

Chapter 10: The promise for your future

To make all of this happen, you have to be willing to defy Sir Isaac Newton! Remember Newton and one of his laws of inertia: "A body at rest tends to stay at rest unless acted upon by an outside force." Inertia, habit, routine, uncertainty, hesitation, fear...all these keep us motionless, keep us from acting on new ideas. If you read about pursuing excellence in your life by becoming an every day person and you don't act upon it, then this book is merely words and scrap paper. Your decision to act becomes that necessary outside force that overcomes inertia. It's time to take action.

Just taking any action is a start but not a finish. One year when I was a staff coach at a camp for high school distance runners, a team from Iowa came to see me after dinner one evening. All seven of their team members were there, and they told me they were on a mission.

"Coach Weinheimer," one of them said, "we want our team to have the same results your team has. Would you be willing to share with us everything your team does?"

Yes, I was willing to do that. Every night after dinner that week, I sat down with the Iowa team and talked about all the aspects of our distance training program. The Iowa kids had their notebooks out and took complete notes on everything that was said. Concerning our training program, I especially emphasized the importance of our weekly Thursday run, a run where our team members basically run as far as they can and as fast as they can. It's a workout that is very tough, very uncomfortable, very tiring, but it is the major building block to our foundation of aerobic capacity. Every other day of the week is built to make Thursday as long as possible and as fast as possible. Our runners tend to dread that workout, but when it is over, they are almost joyful in the knowledge that they have responded to and conquered a great challenge. The Iowa team left camp knowing exactly what our team does that leads to its achievements.

One year later on the first day of camp I looked up the Iowa team and asked them how the previous season had gone for them. Their reply: "Coach Weinheimer, those workouts didn't work for us the way they work for your runners."

That didn't seem to make sense, so I asked a follow up question about the foundation workout. "Tell me about Thursdays. What did you do on Thursdays?"

"Nothing unusual," one answered. "We just did a normal distance run."

"What," I stammered a little, "what happened to the long, fast, hard run?"

"We tried that once or twice. No one liked it, so we stopped doing it and did something easier."

Their season had been doomed by the curse of Isaac Newton and their refusal to overcome inertia and leave their zone of comfort.

Creating a sense of purpose, developing a positive attitude, and following through to the end may not be an easy thing. You are going to decide if you are willing to be uncomfortable in making this change.

Set aside time for thought today. Discover your purpose. Wake up to it tomorrow and every day after. Focus on it. Live it. Return to it during challenging times. Make this Day #1 in your commitment to being an every day person.

Remember Kyle Burton, the creator of the 15 Minute Rule? Kyle has also created a plan sheet that has helped him be cognizant of what his purpose is, what personal qualities it takes to achieve that purpose, and which of those qualities he needs to work to improve. A sample of his plan sheet is included in the pages after the final chapter of this book. You should be able to adapt his ideas no matter what your purpose is.

Stay aware that you are fighting the culture around you, the negative, reactive, look-for-something-easier culture. There will be challenges, obstacles, and "crises." Understand that you will need commitment, especially during those tough moments. Recognize that you are in a process and on a journey. Reward yourself for each day of your "every day."

Challenge yourself to follow through. A different year at that same summer running camp, the coaches talked all week about runners making the decisions to be uncomfortable and to push through tiring times. On the last day of the camp was a four-stage race, each stage separated with a short period of rest. This was the culmination of the entire camp.

I eagerly watched the runners put what they had learned into practice. Effort, sweat, pumping legs, and bright eyes filled the race. As everyone lined up after the short break between stage two and stage three, I noticed two girls who sat down off to the side. I walked over and asked them if they were ready for the next step.

"No. We're exhausted. We're done running for the day."

"C'mon," I prodded, "I think you can finish this race."

"No, Coach, we're done."

This was an affront to my educator ego. My career is all about helping young people realize they can do more than they think they can. I know how to handle this. So I pushed further, "I know you have it in you. Think about why you came to camp. I know you can finish."

I waited. Their reply wasn't verbal. Their heads stayed down, eyes staring at the road, ignoring my presence. I heard their message clearly. Before I could think of what to try next, I heard, "Go" shouted, and the third step of the race began without these girls.

What a disappointment, one that seemed to nullify so much of the message of that week, and one that showed me the limitations of my approach. Learning from that experience, the following year's camp reflected extra support, not only in our traditional learning sessions but also in specific runs throughout the week to prepare for the last morning. The preparation and support paid off. Every runner finished all four stages of the race on the last day.

Words are merely words until they are put into action. Even when you are tired, you have to get back on the starting line. If you have a setback, forgive yourself and return to your foundation. Remember, you never know when the best moment of your day is going to happen.

Even times of great success and achievement may cause your focus to waver. Keep your purpose written where you can see it. Reference it often.

We are all battling Isaac Newton and our personal inertia, often needing our minds to become the outside force that compels us to action. The results are worth it when we can get ourselves out of the comfort zone.

One year at our team cross-country camp at a nearby state park, our seniors were wondering how to get our 100 runners to interact more with each other in spite of their diversity, boys and girls, from 9th graders to 12th graders, from 14 year olds to 18 year olds. On the common campsite where the runners eat, socialize, and take notes during learning sessions, their camp chairs are pushed into makeshift rows. On the first day when setting up the area, the runners plop their chairs down as closely as possible to their best friends, seeking a tiny bit of comfort in the midst of the forest. Seniors sit near seniors and juniors by juniors, but even the classes are segregated within themselves as the freshmen choose to sit only by the freshmen from their same middle school. This arrangement is not unexpected, but it certainly underscores how programmed we are to find our comfort.

Thus the seniors, most aware of the need for team unity, realized the dilemma. How could they build team spirit? How could the team overcome the inertia of runners just hanging out with those others they felt the most comfortable around?

Our seniors talked together and came up with an idea: What would happen if they moved all the chairs so the runners would all be surrounded by new people?

Early the next morning before the rest of the camp woke up, The Great Chair Switch happened. The seniors shuffled all the chairs around, including their own, and then watched as runners woke up, left their tents, and slowly wandered onto the common campsite. Bleary eyed and yawning, everyone seemed to freeze when they saw the change. At first there was consternation, then slow realization, and then a chaotic scene as runners tried to find their own chairs in a new spot ("Is my chair red?"), tripping over each other, bumping elbows, and then widespread giggles when one senior loudly announced, "I can't even find *my own* chair!"

Compliance came reluctantly for several, yet all the runners obediently sat in newly "assigned" places. It was a quiet morning.

Then, over the next few hours, the transformation happened. Eating with a new group, taking notes, laughing, playing cards, telling jokes, having conversation...and by the end of the day the difference in the interaction and noise level was significant, sounding more like a very large family, a bonding experience that carried on throughout the rest of the season.

Three months later in the final junior varsity race, two of our runners, a senior and a freshman, made the final turn side by side and both began sprinting as fast as they could toward the finish line. They raced side by side for seventy meters. Right at the finish the freshman leaned slightly ahead and beat the senior.

Both runners stumbled through the finish chute, trying to control their panting. After a brief moment of recovery, the senior rushed to the freshman, threw her arms around her beaming teammate's neck and gasped, "Way to go. What a great finish." An eighteen year old and a fourteen year old rejoicing in each other's effort. In a sports world where most seniors would be angry to be beaten by a freshman, this could only happen because twelve weeks earlier these kids had been willing to overcome inertia, to get out of their comfort areas and to move their chairs.

Maybe these seniors moved more than their own chairs. Maybe they have inspired more than their teammates; maybe they have inspired us.

Be purposeful and intentional. Embrace the journey toward every day excellence in your life.

> Wake up with a purpose.
>
> Show up with an attitude.
>
> Finish up with a flourish.
>
> Wrap it up with compassion.
>
> And always be willing to move your chair.

Put it into action

Foreword: Your life's defining moments

What events in your life have defined who you are today?

_____

_____

_____

_____

_____

What beliefs do you now hold that have resulted from each of these moments?

Which of these is your one defining moment?

Personal reflections:

Chapter 1: Your purpose for reading

Why are you reading this book?

_____

_____

_____

In what ways would you like your life to be different?

_____

_____

_____

What two thoughts or sentences in chapter 1 stood out to you?

_____

_____

_____

_____

_____

Personal reflections:

Chapter 2: Being aware of the negative

What examples of negativity discussed in chapter 2 do you see around you?

_____

_____

_____

What examples do you see that weren't mentioned?

_____

_____

_____

What events occur during your day that bring the most negativity?

_____

_____

_____

How will you feel when you are able to control those negative thoughts and feelings?

_____

_____

Personal reflections:

Chapter 3: Brick by brick

Where have your deepest-held beliefs come from?

_____

_____

_____

What are the three most important beliefs you have about your life?

_____

_____

_____

What are the three most important beliefs you have about the world?

Personal reflections:

Chapter 4: Naming your purpose

List the things you do almost every day

_____   _____

_____   _____

_____   _____

_____   _____

Which of these are most significant or important?

_____

_____

_____

What would you commit yourself to if you only had time for one thing?

_____

What would you like to be known for?

_____

_____

What one phrase or one statement is the philosophy you are willing to wake up with and commit to every day?

_____

_____

Do you answer "yes" to these three questions?

1. Does this purpose represent the person I want to be?

2. Is the fulfillment of this purpose within my control?
3. Will my commitment to this purpose lead me to go to bed satisfied and wake up motivated to continue the journey?

Personal reflections:

Chapter 5: Getting the attitude

What tasks in your life would you like to turn from "have to" into "get to"?

What are the moments of your day when it is hardest to stay positive?

What specific phrases can you say to yourself when negativity strikes?

_____

_____

_____

When going to bed and looking back on your day, what will a positive day have looked like to you?

_____

_____

_____

Personal reflections:

Chapter 6: Running hard to the end

What are your personal "sticking points" that tempt you to coast near the end of a day or a week?

_____

_____

_____

What will you do specifically to remind and encourage yourself to "finish with a flourish"?

_____

_____

_____

What will finishing strong enable you to accomplish or experience that you would have otherwise missed? What will you be proud of?

_____

_____

_____

_____

_____

Personal reflections:

Chapter 7: Working with others

What specific strategies can you use to help others develop...

Purpose

_____

_____

_____

Positive attitude

_____

_____

_____

The will to finish strong

_____

_____

_____

How will these new skills benefit the lives of those you work with?

_____

_____

_____

Personal reflections:

Chapter 8: Tough times

What times do you anticipate that could test your resolve?

_____

_____

_____

_____

Where will you seek strength in those toughest times?

_____

_____

In what ways can you make a difference in the tough times that other people face?

_____

_____

_____

_____

_____

Personal reflections:

Chapter 9: Eight minute opportunities

What small moments of compassion have you observed in the past few days?

_____

_____

_____

_____

What acts of compassion have you performed for others?

_____

_____

_____

_____

_____

What situations do you anticipate tomorrow when you could show compassion to others in brief moments?

_____

_____

_____

Personal reflections:

Chapter 10: Your future

What things from this book will you immediately do tomorrow?

_____

_____

_____

_____

_____

What will you need to spend more time reflecting on?

_____

Specifically, how will your life be different?

_____

_____

_____

_____

_____

Personal reflections:

Understanding the qualities of your Purpose (plan sheet)

Sample purpose: To become a great coach

(from Kyle Burton)

Necessary Qualities	Qualities I have	Qualities to develop
Knowledge	Training basics	Advanced nutrition, recovery
Patience	Good with others	For myself
Understanding		Listening better
Toughness	My strength!	
Communication	Social media	1-to-1 in person

What would this plan sheet look like for *your* purpose?

How would it bring more focus to your day?

Plan sheet: Your purpose

_____

Necessary Qualities	Qualities I have	Qualities to develop	

Acknowledgements

I am thankful for and grateful to:

My editors—my sister Annie and my mentor Elise; the D.M.A. group (Don't Mention Age) at Asbury United Methodist Church, for suggesting that I write a book; all my English students and runners since 1978; my administrators, principals, assistant principals, and athletic directors; my teaching colleagues at North and Northside; my coaching colleagues through the years and distance coaches from other schools who have become my friends; all the Paavo coaches, especially the 4 Amigos and the Milan Man; Phil, my "oldest" mentor; Chuck, the Fruit Loops story was for you; Perk, for encouragement and showing the way; Mom, the real writer in the family; Jeff; David; Megan; Ian; Kate; Claire; Dave; Gracie; Amy, for always believing this would happen, and for everything else; Glen Lake, for being the only place where the first draft could have been written.

And most of all God, for pointing me in this fulfilling direction.

About the Author

Rick Weinheimer has been a teacher, a coach, and a mentor for almost forty years. He is currently an English department chair in Columbus, Indiana, where he teaches classes, supervises twenty-six teachers, and oversees curriculum for over 2,800 students. Rick was recognized as the Education Hall of Fame recipient for his school corporation in 2014.

As a coach, Rick has led his boys' and girls' cross-country teams to multiple state championships and to national recognition. He has been named Indiana Coach of the Year nine times and has been a four-time nominee for National Coach of the Year. Rick was inducted into the Indiana Association of Track and Cross Country Hall of Fame in 2004.

Rick and his wife Amy, a pre-school special education teacher, have five grown children—David, Megan, Kate, Claire, and Dave—a son-in-law Ian, and a two-year old granddaughter (the Amazing) Grace.

In addition to teaching and coaching, Rick is active as a speaker and workshop coordinator around the country in the topics presented in this book: Purpose, Attitude, Philosophy, Excellence, Leadership, and Compassion. His message is one of inspiration, motivation, and humor.

You can contact Rick through his website: www.rickweinheimer.com.

Made in the USA
Lexington, KY
04 December 2015